BIRDS ON YOUR STREET

BIRDS ON YOUR STREET

by SEYMOUR SIMON

PICTURES BY JEAN ZALLINGER

Holiday House · New York

For Joyce

Text copyright © 1974 by Seymour Simon
Illustrations copyright © 1974 by Jean Zallinger
All rights reserved
Printed in the United States of America

LIBRARY OF CONGRESS CATALOGING IN PUBLICATION DATA

Simon, Seymour.
  Birds on your street.

  (His Science on your street books)
  SUMMARY: Outlines the many things that can be
learned about birds by observing the habits and
characteristics of common city birds.
    1. Birds—Juvenile literature. [1. Birds]
I. Zallinger, Jean Day, illus. II. Title.
QL676.2.S56   598.2   73–17061
ISBN 0–8234–0237–1

HOW TO USE THIS BOOK

Birds on Your Street was written with the idea of helping you to find out about your surroundings. Perhaps the book will show you some new ways of looking at things and thinking about them. Even familiar objects on your street can become new and exciting when you learn how to explore them in different ways.

Scientists need to know more than just facts. They need to know how to go about getting the facts. That's what this book is really about—the methods that scientists use and that you can use too.

By reading the book and following its suggestions you will learn to observe and measure carefully. You will group similar things together in a way that makes thinking about them easier. You'll begin to use numbers and also ideas about size and shape. You'll see how things change with the passage of time. You'll think about what you see and make predictions about what will happen. In short, you'll work in a scientific way.

New discoveries in science come along every day. But the basic skills, the processes of science, continue in the same ways as before. We hope these skills will open new worlds for you to explore wherever you go, even on your own street.

Of all the animals that live on your street,
birds are probably the most familiar to you.
You can watch birds from your window
or when you go out for a walk.

Does your street have many birds?
Where do you look to find them?
Look for birds walking on the ground.
Look for birds on roofs or window ledges.
Look for birds perched on the branches of trees.
Most of all, look for birds flying.

Do all the birds on your street fly in the same way?
Do some birds flap their wings more rapidly than others?
Do some birds glide through the air
without much flapping at all?
Watch how a bird uses its wings and body
to take off and land.
Some long-time bird watchers can tell
one kind of bird from another
by the way it flies.
After watching the birds on your street,
can you see any differences in their flight?

What else are the birds doing?
Look for birds feeding and drinking.
Did you ever see a bird bathing in a puddle of water
after a rain?

A bird also keeps its feathers clean
by preening itself with its bill.
In the spring, you may see a bird building a nest
or caring for its young.

Listen for the sounds that birds make.
Do birds chirp more often during
the hours of early morning and early evening
than during midday?
Do birds chirp during the night?
What do you think most birds do at night?

Do you know what kinds of birds live
on your street?
The first bird you may learn to recognize is the pigeon.
A pigeon is probably the largest bird on your street.

Is a pigeon as large as your hand?
As large as your foot?
How large?
Use a ruler to measure an object
that you think is as large as a pigeon.
How many inches tall did you measure?
You can tell a pigeon by its large size,
its strutting walk, and the cooing sound it makes.

Pigeons may be different colors
but are most often some shade of gray.
They usually have a band of shiny feathers
around their necks.

Perhaps someone on your street has a pigeon roost on a roof.
The pigeons are trained to find their way
back to their roost from a great distance.
At one time, trained pigeons were used to carry messages.
Nowadays, people raise homing pigeons
for racing, or just for fun.

Many people like to feed pigeons by
scattering seed on the ground.
Soon a crowd of pigeons gathers round.
Some people don't like to put out food for pigeons.
They say the food brings rats and mice.
A lot of pigeons nesting on a ledge
will make a building dirty with their droppings.

Starlings are also common city birds.
They are smaller than pigeons.
Try measuring starlings by comparing them
to a familiar object and then measuring the object with a ruler.

A starling may change color from winter to spring.
You can tell an adult starling in the spring
by its dark shiny feathers and yellow beak.
Young starlings are grayish, with many white spots
and a black beak.

Starlings walk along with a quick step.
Their voices are loud and harsh,
but starlings can also whistle, squeak, squeal,
and even imitate the sounds of other birds.
Starlings may make a nest anyplace they find a hole.

You will often see large flocks of starlings feeding together.
Starlings eat almost anything:
seeds, worms, insects, and leftover table scraps.
Look at the shape of a starling's beak.
Why is the shape a good one for poking around in the ground?

Robins are a bit larger than starlings.
You can easily tell them by their
reddish breast and dark gray back.

You'll most often find them looking for
worms and insects on grassy areas
in parks or vacant lots.

Robins hop rather than walk along the ground.
Robins build nests of grass and mud
above the ground in a tree or on the ledge of a building.

Sparrows are small brown birds that travel in groups.
They eat grain and seeds
and bread crumbs that people leave.
Look at the shape of a sparrow's beak.
Do you know why it's just right for cracking seeds?

At one time, horses were used in cities
to carry people from place to place.
There were lots of sparrows then.
Can you tell why?

Hint: Horses eat oats and other grains.

Sparrows make nests of grasses, leaves, and twigs
in trees or buildings.
You can tell a sparrow by its small size,
brown color, the black bars on its feathers,
and a light-colored underside.

City sparrows may be too dirty
for you to see all their markings.

Other birds that you might see on your street
are grackles, blue jays, and catbirds.
Grackles are even larger than pigeons.
They are shiny black with a V-shaped tail.

Blue jays are easy to tell by their
bright blue color and crested head.

Blue jays are large birds with loud voices.
They will drive other birds away from
any bird feeders on your street.

Catbirds are slate gray with a black cap.
They are a bit larger than starlings.
You may not see catbirds as often as you hear them.
Their song is a squeaky one
that always contains cat-like meows.
You'll hear catbirds singing at night
or early in the morning.

Sometimes you'll see still other birds
on your street.
If you live near an ocean or a large lake
you probably see gulls fly high overhead.
Gulls keep lakes and shores clean by eating garbage.
They make nests on islands and other places
where there are not too many people to disturb them.
Look at a gull's feet.

Can you tell what helps it get around so well in the water?

In the spring and fall, you may see
high-flying geese in a **V**-shaped flock.
They are on their way to their seasonal feeding places.
Be on the lookout for different birds that pass by.

Here are some important things to notice about a bird.
Is the bird you are looking at
smaller than a robin, or the same size as a robin,
or bigger than a robin?

What color is the bird?
What does its foot look like?
What kinds of tracks does it make?

PERCHING

HAWK

Does it fly in a straight line,
or up and down, or high up in the sky?

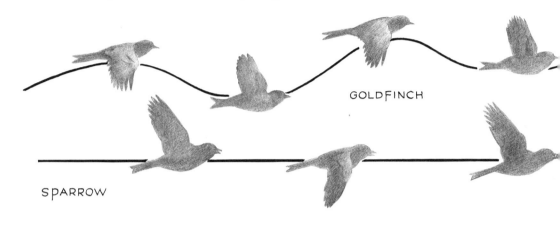

GOLDFINCH

SPARROW

Does it walk or hop along the ground?
What does the bird eat?

Draw a picture showing the shape of its beak.
Do you see the bird all the year round
or only during one season?
Try to draw a picture of the bird,
or photograph it if you have a camera.
It's fun to keep a record of the different birds you see.

One way you can get near enough
to watch birds closely
is to use a bird feeder.
You can make a simple feeding tray.
Use a flat piece of wood for the bottom.
Nail strips of wood around the edges.
Place the tray on a window ledge
or some other place where you can see it easily.
Make sure to choose a place where a cat
can't surprise the birds.

What kinds of foods do birds eat?
Some birds eat worms, insects, and other animal foods.
Other birds eat seeds, grain, and other plant foods.
Still other birds eat both plant and animal foods.
Observe the birds on your street,
and put out the kinds of foods you have seen them eat.
Try sunflower seeds, bits of fat from meat,
dried bread, leftover breakfast cereals,
peanut butter on a cracker, and table scraps.
If you like, you can purchase bird seed
in a pet store or market.

BIRD SEED

Do birds come to your feeder right away?
What happens after the first bird comes?
Do certain birds feed together?
Do some birds drive others away?
Do the same birds come back day after day?
Each day replace the foods that are eaten.
Which foods are eaten first?
Do all the birds eat the same foods?
Even if you can't use a bird feeder,
you can still sprinkle seeds and crumbs
on your windowsill.

Still another good way to attract birds
is to set out a pan of fresh water
on your windowsill.

Make sure the pan can't be upset easily.
Each day clean the pan and change
the water.
You may be surprised to see how
many birds come to drink and bathe.

Spring is a good time to look for bird's nests on your street.
Look up for nests in trees, in chimneys, on ledges
and other high places.
Why is it unlikely that city birds
should build nests on the ground or on low spots?

Make sure not to collect or disturb nests.
Can you tell why not?

Some of the nests you see high in trees
may be squirrels' nests.
Squirrels build nests of leaves and twigs.
Birds may use twigs, leaves, mud, feathers, grass,
and also paper, yarn, string, and bits of cloth
to build their nests.

You could supply a little pile
of some of these during nest-building-time
in the spring.
Nearby your feeding tray or water pan,
spread out some pieces of string, yarn, and
bits of other soft materials.

Do all the different kinds of birds that come to visit
take the nesting supplies?
Which kinds are taken first?
Which are not taken at all?
Perhaps you can examine an *old* deserted bird nest
in school or in a nature club.
What kinds of materials were used in building the nest?
Do you think all birds' nests look the same?

You may be lucky enough to spot a nest
in which birds are sitting on their eggs.
Adult birds sit on their eggs to keep them warm
so that they can hatch.
Watch to see if the parent birds take turns
sitting on their eggs.

Are the eggs ever left alone?
Check each day to see if any changes take place.
One day, you may see great activity around the nest.
The eggs are starting to hatch.
When the baby birds break through the shells,
they start to make peeping sounds right away.
How many babies do you see in the nest?
How do the parents feed the young?
Do both parents bring food back to the nest?
What do the young birds look like at first?
Do they look like their parents when they hatch?
When do you suppose they will look like their parents?
How often are the babies fed?

Each day the baby birds grow bigger and louder.
Soon they will grow feathers and be able to leave the nest.
Do they know how to fly from the beginning?
Are the young taught to fly by the parents?
Watch to see what happens as the
babies leave their nest on their first flight.

Does the nest remain in use for a long time
after the young have learned to fly?
Why do you think spring is the best time for egg laying?
What do you think would happen if the eggs were laid
in fall or winter?

The birds you see on your street are wild animals
that have learned to live near people.
You can find out a great deal about the birds on your street
by watching and listening—
and thinking about what you've observed.